Backyard Wonders

written by
Nancy MacCoon

illustrations by
Courtney Watkins

Published by
Vibatorium
www.vibatorium.com

To purchase this book online:
www.backyardwonders.com

Library of Congress
Control Number 2003116265
ISBN 097424950-5

First Edition

Printed in China

chapter one

HAVE YOU EVER WONDERED ABOUT SOW BUGS?

You see these little flat, gray, crawly sow bugs in the garden whenever you lift up a rock or log. They seem so clean and mild-mannered that your curiosity might cause you to pick one up. Immediately, it rolls up into a ball. That's its defense, how it protects itself from danger. If you are quite still, it will unroll again and explore the near territory, your hand.

While it wanders about your hand, look at it. Don't worry. It doesn't even tickle much. Its body has seven joints. It has seven pairs of walking legs. On the head is a pair of feelers or antennae with very tiny eyes. These eyes have many lenses so that they can detect the slightest motion. At the other end, behind the seventh pair of legs, are flat little plates. These are in the same position as a turtle's tail would be. The bug breathes with these. If the bug were a water animal, these would be called gills.

We've been talking about this as a bug, but a bug is an insect. The sow bug claims a much grander name of Crustacean (Kru-STA-shun). It belongs to the same family as the shrimp, lobster, and crab. They are all Crustacea. The sow bug is of the order or sub-group Isopoda (I-so-POD-a) and has a wonderful name of Armadillidium vulgare (Arm-a-dil-li-DI-um vul-GA-re). If you had a name like that, would you settle for being called "Bug?"

The sow bug is also called pill bug and roly-poly. It eats small, rotting pieces of plants. It won't bite you. It even helps break down vegetable matter in the garden which makes the soil richer.

If this little creature is still in your hand, turn it over. You'll get its pill form but then as it unrolls, keep it on its back. This way you can see the segments clearly. You may even have a female in your hand. If so, the underside will be covered by overlapping plates which form a brood pouch. That's where her babies are kept as eggs and after they are born.

There might be as many as fifty babies and they are just like the adults, except extremely tiny, more like a grain of sand.

I saw a sow bug produce her babies once. I thought she had exploded. But she went on her way, quite calmly, leaving a small, spreading, moving pile of sand.

There are about 3,000 species (SPE-sees) of isopods, but only half of them have been scientifically described. Their fossils have been found and dated from the Jurassic Period. That's right. Isopods and dinosaurs.

I thought to line up the little round sow bugs to see if I could start a race or a game. Ha! When they unrolled, each just wandered about in its own way. No fear, no anxiety, no scurrying about, and definitely no racing. But I'll bet their relatives really had to run to escape being smashed by the huge feet of the dinosaurs.

chapter two

HAVE YOU EVER WONDERED ABOUT LADYBUGS?

When a ladybug landed on my hand, I dutifully obeyed the tradition and said the rhyme: "Ladybird, Ladybird, fly away home. Your house is on fire, Your children will burn."

Then I worried about the little ladybird beetle. She took heed and hurried off to protect her children. Or so I thought. Isn't that rhyme a mean thing to say to her? A ladybird is also called a ladybug in the United States and a lady beetle in Canada. It got its name in Europe in the Middle Ages, way back before the 1500's. This was long before even your great, great, many great grandparents were born. Because the beetle had such power to save crops, the farmers thought it must be godlike. They named it "Bird of Our Lady," Bird of the Virgin Mary.

The ladybug's crop-saving activity comes about because the ladybug likes to eat the insects that eat our flowers, orange trees, alfalfa. You probably have seen the destructive green aphids lining the stem under a rose bud. They eat the rose and the ladybug comes along and eats the aphids. The

ladybug needs about one thousand aphids each month to live.

You know these little ladybug beetles as red or orange, round, (like a ball cut in half) with short legs and black spots. There are 350 different kinds or species in the United States. The number of spots and the color vary according to its kind. They are insects, of the order Coleoptera (Ko-le-OP-ter-a).

Birds don't like the taste of the ladybugs and so the bright color warns them not even to try to catch them. That's neat protection for the bug, don't you think?

In the spring the ladybug lays as many as one hundred tiny yellow eggs on a leaf near a supply of aphids. After five days, out comes the larvae (LAR-vae), which look like very tiny alligators. One of them will feed on as many as 30 aphids a day. After about three weeks, an adult ladybug has developed. Its spots show up quickly and it

must start at once to find food. It crawls and flies from plant to plant. The flying wings are under colorful, hard capes called elytra (EL-i-tra), and are folded out of sight each time it alights.

The ladybug became famous when it was needed to save the orange groves in California in 1889. By mistake, a cottony-cushion scale insect had been brought in from Australia. It set about to ruin the orange trees. What kept it under control in Australia? The ladybug. "Quick, send us some!" By mail came the needed help. In two years the scale was wiped out.

Ever since, the mail-order business has been delivering ladybugs to everyone who needs their protection. When the farmers decided to use pesticides as something new and quicker, they nearly finished off the ladybugs. They soon learned that nothing replaces the ladybug. Back to mail-order.

No wonder it is considered unlucky to kill the ladybug or injure it. That's why the rhyme. The rhyme continues: "Fly, ladybird, fly! North, south, east or west; Fly to the pretty girl that I love best." There's more help from the ladybug than you thought.

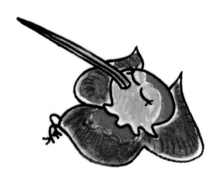

chapter three

HAVE YOU EVER WONDERED ABOUT HUMMINGBIRDS?

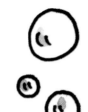

Did you know that hummingbirds like water? If you stand very still near a bird bath, you may see a hummingbird splash about, clean its feathers, and take a bath. This may come as a surprise because hummingbirds are usually seen zipping about amidst flowers, hovering and backing up, but rarely staying still. Hummingbirds are tiny little creatures, most of them no bigger than your thumb. They are noted for quick, perky activity. Their helicopter-like motion of the wings is similar to what we do with our hands and arms when we tread water, only hummingbirds do it much, much faster. Their wings beat between fifty and eighty times each second.

Try flapping your arms as fast as you can. Count. Probably four or five flaps in a second is your best effort.

There are 320 species of hummingbirds in the world and 15 species in the Western Hemisphere. They are of the order Trochiliformes (TRO-kill-i-for-mes). That's a very long name but friends of hummingbirds have given them nick names, such as: coquette, fairy, hill star, sun gem. Perhaps you can think up one of your own.

The hummingbirds all have short legs and small feet. They might be plain brown or in glittery soap-bubble colors but most have a touch of brightness at the throat. Their bills or beaks are long and slender, usually straight, and they are equipped with long tongues which are forked at the tip. With this long beak and tongue, they can collect sweet nectar (flower juice) from the deepest part of the blossom that no other bird can reach. Imagine having an extra long straw to get the very last drop of your favorite drink.

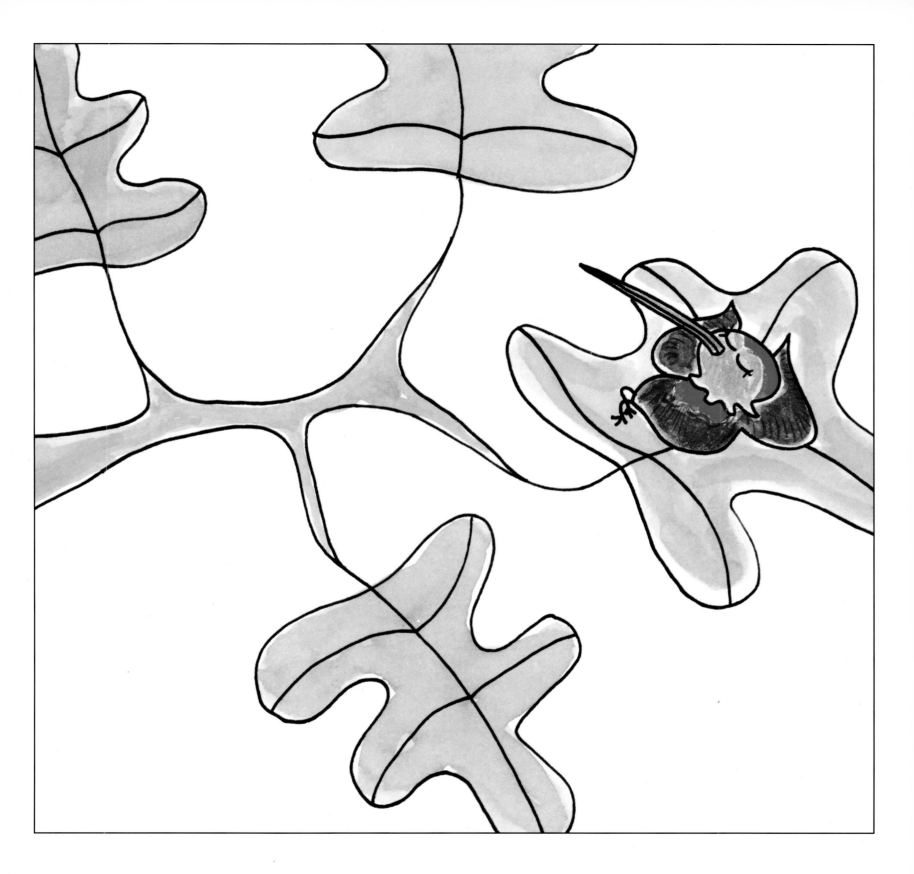

The little hummer is welcome in the garden because it feasts on pests which otherwise would eat the flowers. In addition to the nectar, it likes aphids, small insects, and spiders. It loves red flowers, especially, and hanging red feeders. Hummingbirds have a distinctive flight pattern which is repeated again and again as they watch for food or a likely mate.

They swing like a pendulum, back and forth, humming and squeaking with a high voice. Think about a batch of birds in a band. The hummingbirds would sit in the rhythm section of the band. They have no song, but can make several sounds. Their wings make an underlying hum which gives them their name. Then they add small chirps and peeps that can sound like staccato chatter or the tinkle of a small bell.

You might guess that all the hummer's frantic activity uses up a lot of energy. You're right. It has to hunt for food at least fourteen times each hour. Its body burns up the food almost as fast as it can eat it. To save energy and effort in between spurts of activity, it calms way down, lowers its body temperature, and rests on a tree branch or back at its nest.

The only way you'll see a hummingbird's nest is if the hummingbird leads you to it. It's too well hidden with bits of bark. Through a window covered with red trumpet vine, I watched a little hummer build its nest. It darted back and forth with bits of grass and even spider webs, its long beak pushing and prying at its work until it had a small cup with a folded-in edge to keep the tiny eggs from falling out. The nest measured less than an inch across, about the size of a quarter. In time, I saw two eggs, each smaller than a pea. The eggs hatched in about three weeks.

The wee tiny babies were about the size of my thumbnail. They lifted their bald heads and opened their mouths for food. In another three weeks, they had their feathers and could fly. Very soon after that my hummer family left to explore the huge world out there.

This tiny little bird is a fearless fighter. It attacks hawks or crows, which are many times bigger, and drives them away from the precious eggs. You might imagine a miniature dive bomber with a needle-like beak.

Look around you. Have you seen a hummingbird lately? Now you know where to look. Why not hang a bird feeder high up somewhere or place a bird bath so you can watch the activity. Isn't it astonishing what a wonderful flying machine this little creature is?

chapter four

HAVE YOU EVER WONDERED ABOUT BUMBLEBEES?

Did you know bumblebees give each other high fives? I was watching four bumblebees having a merry time sipping from the tiny purple blossoms on a lavender plant. It seemed to be a sociable picnic. After a sip or two, they would clumsily bump into each other as if giving high fives.

A bumblebee looks like a large honeybee. It is much more peaceful in its lumbering fashion and only stings when frightened or handled. Don't pick one up!

It has a funny defense. If an enemy (a larger bug) attacks, a bumblebee can spit up some honey onto its tongue. It then plasters the enemy, making it very sticky and slow.

The bumblebee is a large hairy insect of the order Hymenoptera (hi-me-NOP-ter-a), the same as a honeybee. It has its own genus, Bombus (BOM-bus). This bee, usually with gold stripes on its black body, is about as large as your thumbnail. It has two sets of wings which seem too small to support such a large body. Common knowledge says that a bumblebee shouldn't be able to fly because of its poor design. It doesn't know that. It flies anyway. Actually, the small wings beat rapidly to make a circular current in the air, called a vortex, which is uplifting.

The bumblebee has the compound eyes of most insects, with its many little lenses. It can see colors that we see and also ultraviolet. It finds its way home by where the sun is, and on a cloudy day, the ultraviolet rays tell the location of the sun. This bee has an especially long tongue to suck up the nectar from the deepest flowers. It collects the yellow pollen and nectar in basket-like holders on the hind legs. When the holders are full, the bee looks as if it has on short baggy pants.

The queen bumblebee comes out of her winter hiding, finds an underground hollow, makes a honeypot filled with nectar, and lays six eggs in her nest. In about four days, the eggs hatch into larvae and then develop into pupae. In two weeks' time, new bees crawl out and feed at the honeypot. Shortly after, they are ready to take up their duties of finding the nectar and pollen to feed the next babies. From then on, the workers nurse the babies, provide the food and clean the nest, while the queen just lays more eggs.

In early fall, new queens are produced and also the drones that will mate with the queens. The size and type of bee is governed by what it is given to eat. The developing queens get special bee milk from a gland in the nurse bee's head.

When it is time for the mating, the new queens fly high up into the sky and the males follow. The strongest male wins the prize. Each queen finds a new winter hiding place and prepares for her job as head of her household the next spring. The old queen and all her workers die.

Farmers are very thankful for bumblebees. In fact, New Zealand farmers were once trying to grow red clover and were failing. Bumblebees were sent over to save the day. They are the only bees with long enough tongues to reach inside the red clover blossom. As the bees travel from flower to flower, their fuzzy bodies get covered with pollen. Some of this pollen drops off onto the next flowers and this way the plants get new pollen and can grow seeds.

One day I saw bumblebees, honey bees, and wasps feasting on the tasty quill ends of bird feathers. They each picked up a feather and carried it to a private lunching place. It looked like a dozen flying feathers, straight up and down, moving through the air.

Have fun watching the bumblebees. Maybe you too can see some high fives and flying feathers.

chapter five

HAVE YOU EVER WONDERED ABOUT FIREFLIES?

My first sight of fireflies was in Williamsburg, Virginia. I found them so enchanting that I could understand why people watched them for hours. There were verandahs or porches almost made for the purpose. Rocking chairs were lined up filled with serene people watching the antics of these little lighted dive bombers.

The firefly, or lightning bug, has been called a traveling night light, a twinkle light, Sparky, a living spark, and even a dancing light. This little bug seems to capture people's imagination. There is a story about the little bug agreeably walking up and down a stick trying to light it for a kid in need of a match. But the little bug failed because he could give only light, not heat. In some countries, lanterns are made with fireflies inside.

On the computer, a man in Houston, Texas, set up a web site to invite firefly watchers to report their spottings. The spottings came in from Japan, Germany, Utah, Colorado, Chico, California, and many places east of the Rocky Mountains. A little girl in Bandera, Texas, came into the house at night with fireflies all over her shirt. She had caught them and put them on her clothing so she could light up.

The fireflies seem to fly in formation quite often, flashing their lights on and off, on and off, as though to an unheard drum.

I could almost see a waltz-time rhythm going for a while.

The flashing light is a courtship tool. The male firefly flashes his light, the female answers back in two seconds. The sender and the receiver keep at it until they meet.

A man in Massachusetts let Sparky loose in the bathroom and Sparky was really confused when he found the light on the man's watch. "What kind of female is this with such a weird signal?" he might have asked.

During the summer months, a firefly might lay as many as 500 eggs on the underside of leaves. After 10 days, they become larvae. The baby or larva gives off light and is called a glowworm. Glowworms eat snails and earthworms. They spend one to two years developing into adults. Glowworms measure about three quarters of an inch, adults are smaller, sometimes less than a half inch in length (a little larger than a ladybug). The adult lives only five to thirty days and will eat nectar or nothing. You can picture an adult firefly sticking around just long enough to find a mate and insure the continuation of its species.

These fireflies are not flies but nocturnal, night-time beetles. They belong to a family, Lampyridae (lam-PEER-e-day) with 2,000 species and turn up all over the world. There are 140 species in the United States and Canada. You'll find them as early as March and as late as October or November. They like warm nights and dampness, and long grasses, bushes, and trees.

This brown or black bug looks as if it is carrying a light bulb at the back, but the light organs are on the underside of the abdomen. These organs consist of layers of mirror-like cells and a layer of light-producing cells which carry nerves and air tubes. The little bug makes the bright soft twinkling light by controlling the flow of air.

By the way, on the lantern idea, a firefly won't glow as brightly in a container and will reward you mightily with a healthy twinkle when you let it go.

Wouldn't it be fun to train these little flying flash lights. Have them sparkle in time to music that we could hear? That's not possible, of course, so just sit back and enjoy their own special brand of fireworks.

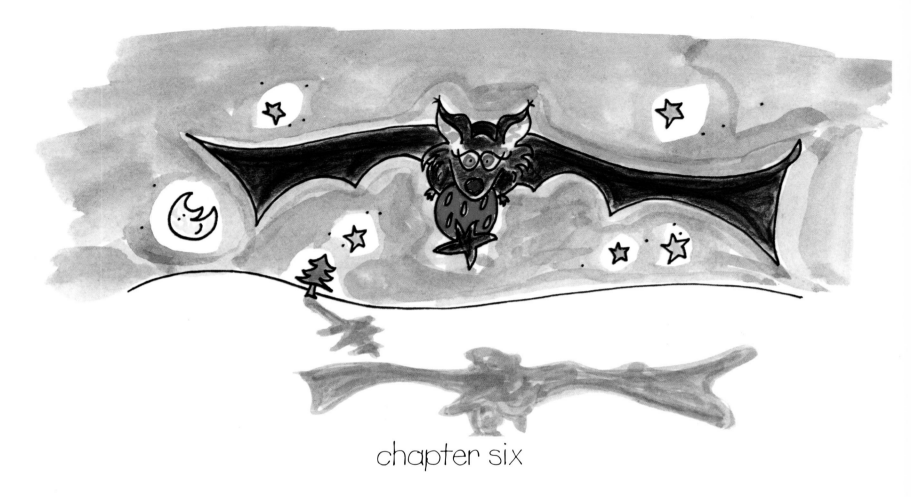

chapter six

HAVE YOU EVER WONDERED ABOUT BATS?

Bats fly like small stunt airplanes. They do flips, sharp turns, and rolls like the plane, but when landing, they're all bat. They grab onto their landing-pad with their feet and hang upside down.

Bats are flying mammals. (A mammal mother nurses her babies.) There are almost 1000 species of bats, of the order Chiroptera (ki-ROP-ter-a). That name means hand wing because their wings are very long fingers connected by a skin or membrane. There is even a thumb which has a claw.

Bats come in all sizes, from crow-sized with a five foot wingspan, to a tiny creature the size of your thumb. The little brown bat is the most common in Canada and the United States. The scary bat, which has given all bats a bad name, is the vampire bat which lives and mostly stays in South America. It is actually quite shy.

Bats hunt for food after dark. The little brown bat eats only insects. It catches them with its wings and tail flap and tosses them into its mouth. How does it find them in the dark? Not with eyes like cats, but with ears that listen, not radar but sonar. Bats have extremely high pitched voices which bounce off the objects around them like echoes. By listening to the echoes, by echolocation, the bat can find his delicious bug and avoid bumping into things.

In the summer, the mother bat has her pup. After two months, it's almost full grown and is on its own.

Bats now have their own fan clubs, Bat Conservation International and Bat World Sanctuary. This is important because bats will disappear unless we help them.

People are still so afraid of them and consider them such a threat to themselves and their farms that they kill them. We need to know that bats are not dangerous when left alone. If a bat has fallen, it might be sick and will bite if you try to touch it. If the bat bites you, the bat must be killed so that it can be tested for rabies. You don't want that. Find an adult and remind him that thick gloves, a can, or dustpan must be used to gently push the bat into a box that can be covered. A Humane Society or Wildlife Group can help you.

But think of this: the bat is a big time helper. The little brown bat can eat up to its weight in mosquitoes in one night. For you to eat your weight in food, you'd have to eat 100 bananas or more at a mealtime. Bats also help carry seeds of plants, and provide a wonderful fertilizer in the form of their droppings or guano.

When no one cared, caves and old mines which had become bats' homes were sealed, trapping bats inside. Now "bat gates" at the mouth of old mines let bats come and go. People are building bat houses, skinny wooden boxes which hang upside down and are open at the bottom.

One Northern California farmer decided to replace the siding on his house. Behind it was a bat colony. The bats flew out, almost knocking him over. After he rebuilt the wall, the bats returned. He built a bat house nearby to help them and raise them so they could protect his crops. Every night a bat would come into his home, cruise around, ignore the cat, squeak a bit, and leave.

Bats groom themselves very carefully, the way cats do. But, while combing with the claws of one foot, they hang upside down by the other foot.

Bats have been raised by researchers and rehabilitators and have become attached to their handlers, purring like cats, and coming on signal. One little flying fox bat learned to wake his caretaker when he wanted food or attention at night. Before he could fly, he would crawl up the covers and poke his care taker's cheek with his wing.

The next time you see a bat, say "Hello," but leave the capturing and training to the professionals. Bat handlers have special shots and special training to heal an injured bat. Remember it is a wild animal and it is illegal in most states to keep wild animals as pets. Because you now know how nice they can be, how helpful and intelligent, you can tell all your friends about them. Be part of a bat fan club.

THE END

Nancy MacCoon is a backyard naturalist with a degree in Zoology and a broad interest in science. She is the mother of two children and has worked with a children's theatre production group for many years. Meticulously researched, this little book recreates the wonderful wide-eyed curiosity of children about every day inhabitants in a garden. This book is designed to stimulate children's interest in nature and at the same time, provide some basic information.

Garnet F. Mason, Ph.D.
Zoology
University of London, England